Mike Curry

Sara Yohe

Kirsten Rogers

Amanda Magnuson

Clare Koppel

Charlie Hall

Joey Larson

Cory Huggar

Justin Hall

Will Harp

Persis Elavia

Caitlin Morris

IDG
BOOKS
WORLDWIDE

IDG Books Consumer Publishing Group
IDG Books Worldwide, Inc.
An International Data Group Company
919 E. Hillsdale Boulevard
Suite 400
Foster City, CA 94404

ISBN: 0-7645-6070-0

GENERAL MILLS, INC.
Betty Crocker Food and Publications Center
Director: Marcia Copeland
Editor: Karen Couné
Food Stylists: Katie W. McElroy, Cindy Syme
Nutrition Department
Nutritionist: Elyse A. Cohen, M.S.
Photographic Services
Photographer: Carolyn Luxmoore

Book design by Michele Laseau

For consistent baking results, the Betty Crocker Food and Publications Center
recommends Gold Medal Flour

Manufactured in the United States of America

10 9 8 7 6 5 4 3 2 1

Cover: (left to right) Ice Cream Sandwiches (page 44), Strawberry Pie (page 76)
Cookies-Sour Cream Cake (page 64)

Contents

Introduction

This baking book was created just for you! You'll learn to bake delicious food, and you'll find it's fun and easy. All recipes were tested by kids to be absolutely sure they work and that they taste terrific.

Baking is very satisfying. First, you can enjoy wonderful smells from the oven, and then, you get to eat what you baked! You'll definitely want to start baking when you read these yummy recipes: Peanut Butter Cookies, Animal Cookies, The Best Brownies, Cookie-Sour Cream Cake, Top-It-Your-Way Pizza, Turtle Bread, Blueberry Streusel Muffins, Snowman Buns, Strawberry Pie, Sugar Cookie Tarts—and more! You'll also find neat ideas, like how to organize a Cookie Exchange, make your own play dough and top your toast in nifty ways.

Be sure to read "Baker's Corner" to learn everything you'll need to know when you're baking. It also explains words that may be new to you and shows the baking equipment you'll be using. And be sure an adult reads the section for them, "For the Baker's Adult Helper."

Always an ask an adult any questions you have before you start to bake. In some recipes, you'll see the words **Adult help**. It's especially important to let your adult helper know when you are baking those recipes so they will be around to help when the recipe calls for them.

Have fun with these recipes! Doing something new can be both creative and rewarding, and you can feel proud when you bake something and serve it for others to enjoy. Try making your favorite recipes, then branch out to new recipes and new taste treats. Learning to bake will give you a lifetime of good fun and good food!

Betty Crocker

Baker's Corner

Let's Get Started!

Before You Start

- Check with an adult to make sure that it's a good time to bake. Also, always let an adult know when your recipe uses the range (stove top).

- If your hair is long, tie it back so it won't get in the way.

- Wash your hands and wear an apron.

- Read the recipe all the way through before starting to cook. Ask an adult about anything you don't understand.

- Gather all the ingredients and utensils before starting to make sure that you have everything. Measure all the ingredients carefully. Put everything you need on a tray. When the tray is empty, you'll know you haven't left anything out!

- Many baked recipes use baking *soda* or baking *powder*, or some of each, as a leavening to make the recipe rise. Pay close attention when reading your recipes so that you do not get these ingredients mixed up.

- Reread the recipe to make sure that you haven't left anything out.

While You Bake

- Clean up as you bake—it makes less work at the end! As you finish using a utensil (except for sharp knives), put it in warm soapy water to soak. Wash sharp knives separately, and be careful of the sharp blades.

Finishing Up

- Wash and dry all the utensils you have used, and put them away. Wash the counters, and leave the kitchen neat and clean.

- Check the range, oven and any other appliances to be sure that you have turned them off. Put away any appliances you have used.

- Leaving the kitchen clean will make everyone glad to have you bake again. Now, enjoy your creation!

Playing It Safe in the Kitchen

Preparing the Food

- Before you use a sharp knife, can opener, blender, electric mixer or the range or oven, be sure that someone older is in the kitchen to help you and to answer questions. Watch for **Adult help:** signs throughout the recipes.

- Always dry your hands after you wash them to avoid slippery fingers.

- Wipe up any spills right away to avoid slippery floors.

- When slicing or chopping ingredients, be sure to use a cutting board.

- Always turn the sharp edge of a knife or vegetable peeler away from you and your hand when you chop or peel foods.

- Turn off the electric mixer or blender before you scrape the sides of the bowl or container so the scraper won't get caught in the blades.

- Turn off the electric mixer and make sure that it's unplugged whenever you put the beaters in or take them out.

- Put large pans on large burners, small pans on small burners. Turn the handles of pots and pans so that they don't stick out over the edge of the range, where they might accidentally be bumped, and make sure that they're not over another burner either.

When You're Baking

- If the racks need to be adjusted higher or lower, be sure to arrange them before you turn on the oven.

- Allow plenty of air space around foods you're baking—no pans or dishes should touch.

- Arrange foods on oven racks so that one isn't placed directly over another.

- Use a tight-fitting lid or aluminum foil when the recipe calls for covering. Uncover cooked foods away from you, and keep your face away from the steam.

- Always use thick, dry pot holders to avoid burns, not thin or wet ones.

- Ask an adult to help you put pans into and take pans out of the oven.

- Ask an adult to help when checking if a recipe is done. Close the oven door quickly when you have finished looking in, so that heat won't be lost.

- Be careful where you put hot pans. Only put them on a surface that is dry and can withstand heat.

For the Baker's Adult Helper

Preparing food for themselves and others is a very satisfying endeavor for children, and children love to bake! There are precautions that must be taught. Your supervision along with some simple rules can make it fun and, more importantly, safe for boys and girls to fix their own snacks and help prepare meals. You are the best judge of the age at which a child should be allowed to use the range, oven, other appliances or sharp knives. Follow these simple steps to help children cook safely:

- Read the recipe all the way through with the child before they start to cook. Explain anything they don't understand.

- We recommend adult supervision whenever children use sharp knives, the range, the oven or small appliances.

- Children should be taught how to correctly set the controls on the range and oven.

- Provide pot holders in a size that's easy for smaller, less adept hands to use.

- Teach children safe food-preparation techniques and how to handle hot foods.

Kitchen Computing

Baker's Talk

Beat: Make smooth with a vigorous stirring motion using a spoon, wire whisk, egg-beater or electric mixer.

Boil: Heat liquid until bubbles keep rising and breaking on the surface.

Chop: Cut food into small, uneven pieces; a sharp knife, food chopper or food processor may be used.

Core: Cut out the stem end and remove the seeds.

Cut in: Mix fat into a flour mixture with a pastry blender using a rolling motion or by cutting with a fork or two knives until particles are size specified.

Dice: Cut into cubes smaller than 1/2 inch.

Drain: Pour off liquid or let it run off through the holes in a strainer or colander, as when draining cooked pasta or ground beef. Or, remove pieces of food from a fat or liquid and set them on paper towels to soak up excess moisture.

Flute: Flatten pastry evenly on rim of pie plate and press firmly around rim with tines of fork.

Grate: Rub against grater to cut into small pieces.

Grease: Spread the bottom and sides of a dish with butter or shortening using a pastry brush or paper towel.

Knead: Curve your fingers and fold dough toward you, then push it away with the heels of your hands, using a quick, rocking motion.

Mix: Combine to distribute ingredients evenly using a spoon, fork, blender or an electric mixer.

Peel: Cut off the skin with a knife or peel with fingers.

Pipe: Press out frosting from a decorating bag using steady pressure to form a design or write a message. To finish a design, stop the pressure and lift the point up and away.

Roll or pat: Flatten and spread with a floured rolling pin or hands.

Utensils You Should Have

For Preparation

Apple corer

Kitchen scissors

Covered rolling pin and board

Biscuit or doughnut cutter

Cookie cutters

Vegetable peeler

Potato masher

Can opener

Decorating bag

Pizza cutter

Pastry blender

Sharp knife

Pastry brush

Ice-cream scoop

Grater

Long serrated knife

Juicer

Small sharp knife

Cutting board

Mixing bowls (set of 3)

Ruler

Custard cups
(6- and 10-ounce)

Timer

Eggbeater

Colander

Strainer

Electric mixer

Wire whisk

For Measuring

Rubber scraper

Liquid measuring cup
(1 cup)

Small spatula

Dry-ingredient measuring
cups (1-, $^1/_2$-, $^1/_3$-, $^1/_4$-cup)

Measuring spoons
($^1/_4$-, $^1/_2$-, 1-teaspoon,
1-tablespoon)

For Top-of-Range Cooking

Tongs

Spatula

**Wooden spoon or
Long-handled spoon with
heatproof handle**

**Saucepans with lids
(2¹/₂- to 3-,
2- and 1-quart**

For Baking

**Loaf pans
(9 × 5 × 3 and
8¹/₂ × 4¹/₂ × 2 ¹/₂ inches)**

9-inch pie plate

Cookie sheet

**Square baking pans
(8 × 8 × 2 and
9 × 9 × 2 inches)**

**Rectangular pan
(13 × 9 × 2)**

**Round layer cake pans
(8 × 1¹/₂ inches and
9 × 1¹/₂)**

**Jelly roll pan
(15¹/₂ × 10¹/₂ × 1 inches)**

Pot holders

Wire cooling rack

Pizza pan (14 inches)

Muffin pan (6-cup)

**Casseroles with lids
(1-, 2- or 3-quart)**

**Tube pan
(10 × 4 inches)**

Measuring Up

All-purpose Flour. Spoon flour lightly into dry-ingredient measuring cup. Level with spatula. Bisquick® baking mix and granulated and powdered sugars are measured the same way.

Baking Powder. Dip and fill measuring spoon. Level with spatula. Baking soda, cream of tartar and spices are measured in the same way. Liquids, like vanilla, can also be measured in measuring spoons.

Chopped Nuts. Pack lightly into dry-ingredient measuring cup. Also measure shredded cheese, soft bread crumbs and shredded coconut this way.

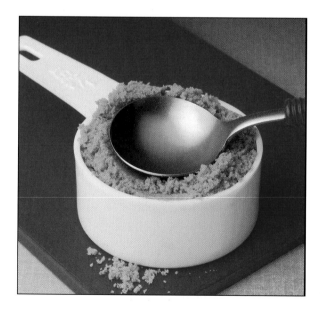

Brown Sugar. Pack firmly into dry-ingredient measuring cup. Level with spatula.

Shortening. Pack firmly into dry-ingredient measuring cup. Level with spatula and remove with rubber scraper.

Molasses and Corn Syrup. Pour into liquid measuring cup. Remove with rubber scraper.

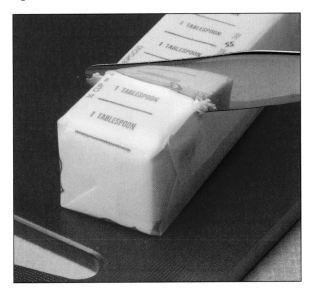

Margarine or Butter. Cut using measurement marks on the wrapper as a guide.

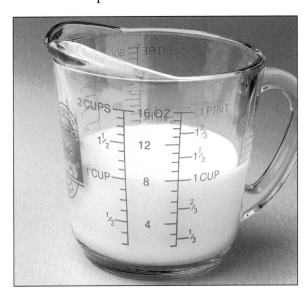

Milk and Other Liquids. Set liquid measuring cup on counter. Pour in the liquid. Bend down to check the correct amount at eye level.

1

▲▲▲▲▲▲▲▲

Crazy About Cookies, Brownies and Bars

Animal Cookies (page 36)

▲▲▲▲▲ "GINGERPOP" COOKIES ▲▲▲▲▲

About 18 cookies

Utensils You Will Need

Large bowl • Liquid measuring cup • Wooden spoons • Plastic wrap •
18 flat wooden ice-cream sticks • Cookie sheet • Glass • Pot holders • Spatula •
Wire cooling rack • Small bowl • Knife

1 Mix in large bowl with wooden
spoon ‑ ‑ ‑ ‑ ‑ ‑ ‑ ‑ ‑ ‑ ►

> **1 package (14.5 ounces) ginger-bread cake and cookie mix
> 1/3 cup lukewarm water**

2 Cover dough with plastic wrap and
refrigerate about 15 minutes or until
slightly firm.

3 Heat oven to 375°.

4 Shape dough into 18 1 1/4-inch balls. Poke 1 ice-cream stick into the side
of each ball until tip of stick is in center of ball. Put balls about 2 inches
apart on cookie sheet.

5 Flatten balls gently with bottom of
glass dipped in ‑ ‑ ‑ ‑ ‑ ‑ ‑ ►

> **Sugar**

6 Bake 8 to 10 minutes or until edges
are firm. Cool cookies on cookie sheet 1 minute, then remove with spatula
to wire rack. Cool completely.

7 Mix in small bowl with wooden
spoon ‑ ‑ ‑ ‑ ‑ ‑ ‑ ‑ ‑ ‑ ►

> **1 cup vanilla ready-to-spread
> frosting
> 2 drops red food color**

8 Spread frosting over each cookie
with knife, then immediately make
face or decorate as you like with ‑ ‑ ►

> **Assorted candies (candy-coated
> chocolate candies, candy corn,
> licorice or gumdrops)**

Nutrition Per Cookie: Calories 155 (Calories from Fat 45); Fat 5g (Saturated 1); Cholesterol 0mg; Sodium 1mg; Carbohydrate 27g (Dietary Fiber 0g); Protein 1g

Although Amanda thought the dough was kind of hard to roll into balls, she also thought it was fun to make and decorate the cookies. And, she said, everyone liked them! We want to assure Amanda that, just like most things, shaping cookie dough does get easier with practice.

HINT

If dough is too soft to shape into balls, cover with plastic wrap and refrigerate about 1 hour. When flattening balls of dough with a glass, you may want to lightly grease the bottom of the glass with shortening to help the sugar stick to the glass.

▲▲▲▲ HOLIDAY HONEY COOKIES ▲▲▲▲

About 42 cookies *(photo page 22)*

Utensils You Will Need

Cookie sheet • Pastry brush • Large bowl • Dry-ingredient measuring cups •
Small sharp knife • Measuring spoons • Wooden spoon • Rolling pin • Ruler •
2-inch cookie cutters • Pot holders • Spatula • Wire cooling rack

1 Heat oven to 375°.

2 Lightly grease cookie sheet with - - - ➤ | **Shortening**

3 Mix in large bowl with wooden
spoon - - - - - - - - - - ➤

| **1/3 cup powdered sugar** |
| **1/3 cup margarine or butter, softened** |
| **2/3 cup honey** |
| **1 teaspoon almond extract** |
| **1 large egg** |

4 Stir in - - - - - - - - - ➤

| **2 3/4 cups all-purpose flour** |
| **1 teaspoon baking soda** |
| **1/2 teaspoon salt** |

5 Sprinkle a clean surface (such as a
kitchen counter or breadboard) with
flour. Put dough on surface. Roll
dough until 1/8 inch thick. Cut with cookie cutters. Put cookies about
1 inch apart on cookie sheet.

6 Bake 6 to 8 minutes or until light brown. Watch carefully because cookies
brown quickly. Immediately remove cookies from cookie sheet with spatula
to wire rack. Cool completely.

7 Frost cookies with - - - - - ➤ | **Glaze (right)**

8 Decorate cookies with - - - - - ➤ | **Decorator's Frosting (right)**

GLAZE Medium bowl • Dry-ingredient measuring cup • Measuring spoons • Wooden spoon

1 Mix in medium bowl with wooden spoon until smooth - - - - - - ➤

> **2 cups powdered sugar**
> **1/4 teaspoon almond extract**
> **2 tablespoons water**

2 Stir in, 1 teaspoon at a time, until spreadable - - - - - - - - ➤

> **2 to 4 teaspoons water**

DECORATOR'S FROSTING Small bowl • Dry-ingredient measuring cup • Measuring spoons • Wooden spoon

1 Mix in small bowl with wooden spoon, adding the water 1 teaspoon at a time, until frosting is thin enough to drizzle or thick enough to be used in a decorating bag - - - - - - - ➤

> **1 cup powdered sugar**
> **3 or 4 drops food color**
> **3 to 5 teaspoons water**

Nutrition Per Cookie: Calories 100 (Calories from Fat 20); Fat 2g (Saturated 0g); Cholesterol 5mg; Sodium 75mg; Carbohydrate 20g (Dietary Fiber 0g); Protein 1g

When we asked Clare to test these cookies, we called them Hanukkah Honey Cookies. While making them, she thought they would be great cut out in any holiday shapes and suggested that we change their name to Holiday Honey Cookies, which we did! Good idea, Clare!

HINT
If dough is too soft to roll, cover with plastic wrap and refrigerate about 2 hours.

▲▲▲▲▲ EASY SUGAR COOKIES ▲▲▲▲▲

About 48 cookies

🍴 Utensils You Will Need

Large bowl • Dry-ingredient measuring cups • Measuring spoons •
Wooden spoon • Cookie sheet • Teaspoon • Glass • Pot holders •
Spatula • Wire cooling rack • Small bowl

1 Heat oven to 375°.

2 Beat in large bowl with wooden spoon until smooth ▬ ▬ ▬ ▬ ▬ ➤

> **1 cup sugar**
> **1 cup (2 sticks) margarine or butter, softened**
> **1/2 teaspoon vanilla**
> **1 large egg**

3 Stir in ▬ ▬ ▬ ▬ ▬ ▬ ▬ ▬ ➤

> **2 1/4 cups all-purpose flour**

4 Shape dough by teaspoonfuls into balls. Put balls about 2 inches apart on cookie sheet.

5 Flatten balls gently with bottom of glass dipped in ▬ ▬ ▬ ➤

> **Sugar, colored sugar or candy sprinkles**

6 Bake 10 to 12 minutes or until set and edges just begin to brown. Cool cookies on cookie sheet 1 minute, then remove with spatula to wire rack. Cool.

Nutrition Per Cookie: *Calories 75 (Calories from Fat 35); Fat 4g (Saturated 1); Cholesterol 5mg; Sodium 45mg; Carbohydrate 9g (Dietary Fiber 0g); Protein 1g*

HINT
If dough is too soft to shape, cover with plastic wrap and refrigerate about 1 hour.

Holiday Honey Cookies (page 20)

▲▲▲▲▲ SANTA CLAUS COOKIES ▲▲▲▲▲

About 30 cookies

Utensils You Will Need

Large bowl • Dry-ingredient measuring cups • Measuring spoons •
Wooden spoons • Ruler • Cookie sheet • Glass • Pot holders • Spatula •
Wire cooling rack • Small bowl • Knife

1 Heat oven to 400°.

2 Mix in large bowl with wooden
spoon ------------➤

> **1 cup granulated sugar**
> **1/2 cup shortening**
> **2 tablespoons milk**
> **1 large egg**

3 Stir in ------------➤

> **2 cups all-purpose flour**
> **1 teaspoon baking powder**
> **1/2 teaspoon baking soda**
> **1/2 teaspoon salt**

4 Shape dough into 1 1/4-inch balls. Put
balls about 2 inches apart on cookie
sheet.

5 Flatten balls until about
2 1/2 inches across with bottom of
glass dipped in ------------➤

> **Sugar**

6 Bake 8 to 10 minutes or until edges are
light brown. Immediately remove cookies from cookie sheet with spatula to
wire rack. Cool completely.

7 For frosting, mix in small bowl
with wooden spoon, adding the water
1 teaspoon at a time, until
spreadable ------------➤

> **1 1/2 cups powdered sugar**
> **1/2 teaspoon vanilla**
> **2 to 3 tablespoons water**

8 To decorate cookies, you will need about - - - - - - - - - - - - - →

3 tablespoons red sugar
1/2 cup shredded coconut
30 miniature marshmallows
60 currants or raisins
30 red cinnamon candies

9 Spread frosting on 1 cookie at a time, then sprinkle red sugar on top third of cookie for hat and sprinkle coconut on bottom third for beard. Press on 1 marshmallow for tassel of hat, 2 currants for eyes and 1 cinnamon candy for nose.

Here's another idea. . . Make **Santa Claus Cookie Pops:** Before baking, poke 1 flat wooden ice-cream stick into the side of each flattened ball of dough until tip of stick is in center of ball.

Nutrition Per Cookie: Calories 135 (Calories from Fat 35); Fat 4g (Saturated 1g); Cholesterol 10mg; Sodium 80mg; Carbohydrate 24g (Dietary Fiber 0g); Protein 1g

GIANT COLORFUL
▲▲▲▲▲ CANDY COOKIES ▲▲▲▲▲

About 18 cookies

Utensils You Will Need

Large bowl • Dry-ingredient measuring cups • Electric mixer • Measuring spoons • Wooden spoon • Cookie sheet • Ruler • Fork • Pot holders • Spatula • Wire cooling rack

1 Heat oven to 375°.

2 Beat in large bowl with electric mixer on medium speed about 5 minutes or until fluffy - - - - - - - ➤

> **1 cup packed brown sugar**
> **3/4 cup granulated sugar**
> **1 cup (2 sticks) margarine or butter, softened**

3 Beat in - - - - - - - ➤

> **1 teaspoon vanilla**
> **2 large eggs**
> **2 1/2 cups all-purpose flour**
> **3/4 teaspoon salt**
> **3/4 teaspoon baking soda**

4 Stir in - - - - - - - ➤

> **2 cups candy-coated chocolate candies**

5 Drop dough by 1/4 cupfuls about 2 inches apart onto cookie sheet. Flatten dough gently with fork.

6 Bake 11 to 14 minutes or until edges are light brown. Cool cookies 3 to 4 minutes on cookie sheet, then carefully remove with spatula to wire rack. Cool.

Here's another idea. . . Make **Giant Chocolate Chip Cookies:** Leave out candy-coated chocolate candies. Stir in 2 cups semisweet chocolate chips instead.

Nutrition Per Cookie: Calories 355 (Calories from Fat 145); Fat 16g (Saturated 5g); Cholesterol 25mg; Sodium 300mg; Carbohydrate 50g (Dietary Fiber 1g); Protein 4g

While testing these cookies, Charlie learned that you should always pack brown sugar when measuring it. His mom showed him how to press it down with the back of a spoon as he put each scoop into the cup.

▲▲▲▲▲ SLICE 'N EASY COOKIES ▲▲▲▲▲

About 66 cookies

🍴 Utensils You Will Need

Large bowl • Dry-ingredient measuring cups • Small sharp knife • Measuring spoons • Wooden spoon • Plastic wrap • Ruler • Sharp knife • Cookie sheet • Pot holders • Spatula • Wire cooling rack

1 Mix in large bowl with wooden spoon ➡

> **1 cup granulated sugar**
> **1 cup packed brown sugar**
> **2/3 cup shortening**
> **2/3 cup margarine or butter, softened**
> **2 teaspoons vanilla**
> **2 large eggs**

2 Stir in ➡

> **3 1/4 cups all-purpose flour**
> **1/2 cup cocoa**
> **1 teaspoon baking soda**
> **1 teaspoon salt**

3 Sprinkle a clean surface (such as a kitchen counter or breadboard) with flour. Put dough on surface. Shape dough into a ball with lightly floured hands, pressing to pack tightly. Cut dough in half. Shape each half into a roll, about 2 inches across and about 8 inches long, by gently rolling dough back and forth on floured surface. Roll dough onto plastic wrap. Wrap plastic wrap around dough and twist ends tightly.

4 Refrigerate rolls at least 8 hours. (Rolls can be refrigerated up to 1 month or frozen up to 3 months.)

5 Heat oven to 375°.

6 Unwrap rolls. **Adult help:** Cut rolls into 1/4-inch slices. (It is not necessary to thaw frozen rolls before slicing.) Put slices about 2 inches apart on cookie sheet.

7 Bake 6 to 8 minutes or until set. Immediately remove cookies from cookie sheet with spatula to wire rack. Cool.

Here's another idea. . . Make **Chocolate Chip Cookies:** Leave out cocoa. Stir in 1 cup miniature semisweet chocolate chips and 1 cup chopped nuts with the flour.

Here's another idea. . . Make **Mint Sandwich Cookies:** Cut refrigerated or frozen rolls into 1/8-inch slices. Bake about 6 minutes or until set. For filling, mix 4 cups powdered sugar, 1/2 cup (1 stick) margarine or butter, softened, and 1 teaspoon mint extract. Stir in 3 to 4 tablespoons water, 1 teaspoon at a time, until smooth and spreadable. Stir in a few drops of green or red food color to tint frosting, if you like. Put cooled cookies together in pairs with mint filling.

Nutrition Per Cookie: Calories 90 (Calories from Fat 35); Fat 4g (Saturated 1g); Cholesterol 5mg; Sodium 80mg; Carbohydrate 12g (Dietary Fiber 0g); Protein 1g

Caitlin has big plans for these easy cookies. She suggests turning them into a super dessert by serving them with a scoop of vanilla ice cream and chocolate sauce on top.

▲▲▲▲▲ ROCKY ROAD COOKIES ▲▲▲▲▲

About 48 cookies

🍴 Utensils You Will Need

1-quart saucepan • Dry-ingredient measuring cups • Wooden spoons •
Small sharp knife • Large bowl • Measuring spoons • Teaspoon • Cookie sheet
• Ruler • Pot holders • Spatula • Wire cooling rack

1 Melt in saucepan over low heat, stirring
a few times, then remove from heat and
cool slightly ▪ ▪ ▪ ▪ ▪ ▪ ▪ ▪ ▪ ▶

2 Heat oven to 400°.

> **1/2 cup semisweet chocolate chips**
> **1/2 cup (1 stick) margarine or butter**

3 Mix in large bowl with wooden
spoon ▪ ▪ ▪ ▪ ▪ ▪ ▪ ▪ ▪ ▶

> **1 1/2 cups all-purpose flour**
> **1 cup sugar**
> **1/2 teaspoon baking powder**
> **1/2 teaspoon vanilla**
> **1/4 teaspoon salt**
> **2 large eggs**
> **1 cup chopped nuts**
> **1/2 cup semisweet chocolate chips**
> **The melted chocolate mixture**

4 Drop dough by rounded teaspoonfuls
about 2 inches apart onto cookie sheet.

5 Press into center of each cookie
1 of ▪ ▪ ▪ ▪ ▪ ▪ ▪ ▪ ▪ ▶

> **About 48 miniature marshmallows**

6 Bake 8 to 12 minutes or until almost no mark stays when cookie is touched. Immediately remove cookies from cookie sheet with spatula to wire rack. Cool.

Nutrition Per Cookie: Calories 95 (Calories from Fat 45); Fat 5g (Saturated 1g); Cholesterol 10mg; Sodium 45mg; Carbohydrate 11g (Dietary Fiber 0g); Protein 1g

Joey thought these cookies were fun to make and especially liked cracking the eggs and pressing the marshmallows into the middle of each cookie.

▲▲▲▲▲ **PEANUT BUTTER COOKIES** ▲▲▲▲▲

About 36 cookies

🍴 **Utensils You Will Need**

Large bowl • Dry-ingredient measuring cups • Small sharp knife • Wooden spoon • Measuring spoons • Plastic wrap • Ruler • Cookie sheet • Fork • Pot holders • Spatula • Wire cooling rack

1 Heat oven to 375°.

2 Mix in large bowl with wooden spoon ▬ ▬ ▬ ▬ ▬ ▬ ▬ ➤

> **1/2 cup granulated sugar**
> **1/2 cup packed brown sugar**
> **1/2 cup peanut butter**
> **1/4 cup shortening**
> **1/4 cup (1/2 stick) margarine or butter, softened**
> **1 large egg**

3 Stir in ▬ ▬ ▬ ▬ ▬ ▬ ▬ ➤

> **1 1/4 cups all-purpose or whole wheat flour**
> **3/4 teaspoon baking soda**
> **1/2 teaspoon baking powder**
> **1/4 teaspoon salt**

4 Shape dough into 1 1/4-inch balls. Put balls about 3 inches apart on cookie sheet. Flatten balls gently in crisscross pattern with fork dipped in sugar.

5 Bake 9 to 10 minutes or until light brown. Cool cookies 2 minutes on cookie sheet, then remove with spatula to wire rack. Cool.

Here's another idea. . . Make **Quick Peanut Butter Sticks**: Divide dough into fourths. Shape fourths into strips, 10 inches long by 1 1/2 inches wide, on cookie sheets. (Two strips can fit on 1 cookie sheet.) Flatten strips to 3 inches wide with fork dipped in sugar. Bake 10 to 12 minutes or until golden brown. Cool 2 minutes, then cut each strip crosswise into 1-inch slices. Remove cookies from cookie sheet with spatula to wire rack. Cool. About 42 cookies.

HINT
If dough is too soft to shape into balls, cover with plastic wrap and refrigerate about 1 hour.

Nutrition Per Cookie: *Calories 90 (Calories from Fat 45); Fat 5g (Saturated 1g); Cholesterol 5mg; Sodium 85mg; Carbohydrate 10g (Dietary Fiber 0g); Protein 1g*

▲▲▲▲▲ CARAMEL-NUT COOKIES ▲▲▲▲▲

About 32 cookies

🍴 Utensils You Will Need

Large bowl • Dry-ingredient measuring cups • Measuring spoons • Wooden spoons • Cookie sheet • Sharp knife • Cutting board • Teaspoon • Pot holders • Spatula • Wire cooling rack • 1-quart saucepan • Knife

1 Mix in large bowl with wooden spoon ▬ ▬ ▬ ▬ ▬ ▬ ▬ ▶

> **1/2 cup packed brown sugar**
> **1/2 (1 stick) margarine or butter, softened**
> **2 tablespoons water**
> **1 teaspoon vanilla**

2 Stir in until dough holds together (if dough is dry, stir in 1 to 2 teaspoons water) ▬ ▬ ▬ ▬ ▶

> **1 1/2 cups all-purpose flour**
> **1/8 teaspoon salt**

3 Heat oven to 350°.

4 To assemble cookies, you will need about ▬ ▬ ▬ ▬ ▬ ▬ ▬ ▶

> **160 pecan halves (about 2 1/4 cups)**
> **8 vanilla caramels, unwrapped**

5 **Adult help:** Cut each caramel into 4 pieces with sharp knife.

6 For each cookie, group 5 pecan halves on cookie sheet (for legs and head of turtle). Shape 1 teaspoon dough around each caramel piece to form a ball. Press ball firmly onto center of each turtle.

7 Bake 12 to 15 minutes or until set but not brown. Immediately remove cookies from cookie sheet with spatula to wire rack. Cool completely.

8 Melt in saucepan over low heat, stirring a few times, then remove from heat ➤

1 ounce unsweetened chocolate

9 Beat into chocolate with wooden spoon, adding the water 1 teaspoon at a time, until smooth ➤

1 cup powdered sugar
1 teaspoon vanilla
2 to 4 teaspoons water

10 Spread tops of cookies with chocolate glaze.

Nutrition Per Cookie: *Calories 115 (Calories from Fat 55); Fat 6g (Saturated 1g); Cholesterol 0mg; Sodium 50mg; Carbohydrate 14g (Dietary Fiber 0g); Protein 1g*

▲▲▲▲▲ ANIMAL COOKIES ▲▲▲▲▲

About 30 cookies *(photo page 17)*

Utensils You Will Need

Large bowl • Dry-ingredient measuring cups • Measuring spoons •
Wooden spoon • Plastic wrap • Tablespoon • Cookie sheet • Pot holders •
Spatula • Wire cooling rack

1 Heat oven to 350°.

2 Mix in large bowl with wooden spoon ▬ ▬ ▬ ▬ ▬ ▬ ▬ ➤

> **1/2 cup granulated sugar**
> **1/2 cup packed brown sugar**
> **1/2 cup (1 stick) margarine or butter, softened**
> **1 teaspoon vanilla**
> **1 large egg**

3 Stir in ▬ ▬ ▬ ▬ ▬ ▬ ▬ ➤

> **2 cups all-purpose flour**
> **1 teaspoon baking powder**
> **1/2 teaspoon salt**
> **1/2 teaspoon ground cinnamon**

4 Shape dough by 2 tablespoonfuls into slightly flattened balls and ropes. Make animal shapes with balls and ropes of dough on cookie sheet.

5 Bake 10 to 12 minutes or until edges are golden brown. Cool cookies 3 minutes on cookie sheet, then remove with spatula to wire rack. Cool.

Here's another idea. . . Make **Letter and Number Cookies**: Make dough as directed. Shape dough by level tablespoonfuls into ropes, about 8 inches long and about 1/4 inch thick. Shape into letters and numbers as desired on cookie sheet. Bake 8 to 10 minutes. About 3 dozen cookies.

Nutrition Per Cookie: Calories 85 (Calories from Fat 25); Fat 3g (Saturated 1g); Cholesterol 10mg; Sodium 90mg; Carbohydrate 13g (Dietary Fiber 0g); Protein 1g

HINT
If dough is too soft to shape, cover with plastic wrap and refrigerate about 2 hours or until firm.

KIDS' HOLIDAY COOKIE EXCHANGE

What could be better than having a holiday party and being with your friends and then when the party is over, you have a bunch of different cookies? That's what a cookie exchange is all about—friends sharing good times and good cookies!

To plan a cookie exchange:

1 Plan the date and time with your parents or an adult who will supervise the event. Decide if you want to send recipes to your friends for them to make or take pot-luck on whatever they want to make.

2 Plan for treats and activities that are appropriate for the weather in your part of the country. If you live where there will be snow, arrange to go sledding or ice skating. If you live in a warmer area, plan to go roller skating or hiking. Indoor activities and games would also be fun.

3 Send invitations to about 5 friends and ask them each to bring a recipe of cookies to the party. You can invite more or fewer kids, depending on your wishes.

4 When it's time to share the cookies, put them all out around a table. Divide each batch of cookies by the number of kids who are at the party. Provide boxes and containers or paper plates and plastic bags and let everyone go around the table and pack up the correct number of cookies to take home.

Cookie Ideas for a Cookie Exchange

Easy Sugar Cookies (page 23)

Santa Claus Cookies (page 24)

Slice 'n Easy Cookies (Chocolate Chip Variation) (page 28)

Caramel-Nut Cookies (page 34)

Double Mint Brownies (page 48)

Peanut Butter and Jam Bars (page 50)

Cookie Exchange—Easy Sugar Cookies (page 23), Santa Claus Cookies (page 24), Slice 'n Easy Cookies (page 28), Peanut Butter and Jam Bars (page 50)

▲▲▲▲▲ **BUMBLEBEES** ▲▲▲▲▲

About 48 cookies

Utensils You Will Need

Large bowl • Dry-ingredient measuring cups • Liquid measuring cup • Wooden spoon • Measuring spoons • Plastic wrap • Ruler • Cookie sheet • Pot holders • Spatula • Wire cooling rack

1 Mix in large bowl with wooden spoon ⇒

> **1/2 cup peanut butter**
> **1/2 cup shortening**
> **1/3 cup packed brown sugar**
> **1/3 cup honey**
> **1 large egg**

2 Stir in ⇒

> **1 3/4 cups all-purpose flour**
> **3/4 teaspoon baking soda**
> **1/2 teaspoon baking powder**

3 Cover dough with plastic wrap and refrigerate about 2 hours or until firm.

4 Heat oven to 350°.

5 Shape dough into 1-inch balls. (Dough will be slightly sticky.)

6 To assemble cookies, you will need about ⇒

> **8 dozen pretzel twists**
> **8 dozen pretzel sticks**

7 For each cookie, put 2 pretzel twists side by side on cookie sheet, with rounded sides touching. Put 1 ball of dough in center, and flatten gently.

8 Break 2 pretzel sticks in half. Gently press 3 pretzel stick halves into dough for stripes on bee. Break last pretzel piece in half. Poke pieces in 1 end of dough for antennae.

9 Bake 11 to 13 minutes or until light golden brown. Immediately remove cookies from cookie sheet with spatula to wire rack. Cool.

Nutrition Per Cookie: Calories 85 (Calories from Fat 35); Fat 4g (Saturated 1g); Cholesterol 5mg; Sodium 120mg; Carbohydrate 11g (Dietary Fiber 0g); Protein 1g

Bumblebees, Super Snack Bars (page 49)

▲▲▲▲▲ MULTIGRAIN CUTOUTS ▲▲▲▲▲

About 70 cookies

Utensils You Will Need

Large bowl • Dry-ingredient measuring cups • Liquid measuring cups •
Measuring spoons • Wooden spoon • Rolling pin • Ruler • Cookie cutters •
Cookie sheet • Decorating bag • Pot holders • Spatula • Wire cooling rack

1 Heat oven to 350°.

2 Mix in large bowl with wooden spoon ▬ ▬ ▬ ▬ ▬ ▬ ➤

> **1 cup sugar**
> **2/3 cup shortening**
> **3 1/4 cups whole wheat flour**
> **1/4 cup cornmeal**
> **1/4 cup wheat germ**
> **3/4 cup milk**
> **1 teaspoon baking powder**
> **1/2 teaspoon salt**
> **1/2 teaspoon vanilla**

3 Sprinkle a clean surface (such as a kitchen counter or breadboard) with flour. Put dough on surface. Divide dough into 3 parts. Roll 1 part of dough at a time until 1/8 inch thick. Cut dough with cookie cutters. Put cookies on cookie sheet.

4 Put in decorating bag with #5 writing tip and outline or decorate unbaked cookies with ▬ ▬ ➤

> **Baked-on Frosting (right)**

5 Bake 12 to 14 minutes or until edges are light brown. Cool 1 minute on cookie sheet, then remove with spatula to wire rack. Cool.

BAKED-ON FROSTING Small bowl • Dry-ingredient
measuring cup • Small sharp knife • Wooden spoon • Measuring spoon

1 Mix in small bowl with wooden spoon until smooth ➔

> **2/3 cup all-purpose flour**
> **2/3 cup margarine or butter, softened**

2 Stir in, 1 teaspoon at a time, until spreadable ➔

> **3 to 4 teaspoons hot water**

Nutrition Per Cookie: Calories 70 (Calories from Fat 35); Fat 4g (Saturated 1g); Cholesterol 0mg; Sodium 45mg; Carbohydrate 9g (Dietary Fiber 1g); Protein 1g

HINT
If you don't have a decorating bag, you can make one with a plastic bag or paper envelope. Put frosting in the corner of a plastic bag and seal, or put frosting in the corner of an envelope and fold the other end over. Snip a small piece off the corner of the bag or envelope to make a writing tip.

Will had fun making and eating this healthy snack. His younger brothers and sister helped cut out some of the shapes.

ICE-CREAM SANDWICHES

About 18 sandwich cookies

Utensils You Will Need

Tablespoon • Dry-ingredient measuring cup • Measuring spoon • Rectangular pan, 13 × 9 × 2 inches • 1-quart saucepan • Wooden spoon • Plastic wrap

1 Make and let cool - - - - - - - → **Peanut Butter Cookies (page 32)**

2 To assemble ice-cream sandwiches, you will need about - - - - - → **2 cups ice cream (any flavor), slightly softened**

3 For each ice-cream sandwich, press 1 rounded tablespoon ice cream between 2 cookies. Put sandwiches in rectangular pan and freeze uncovered about 1 hour until firm.

4 If you like, roll the edges of the sandwiches in - - - - - - - → **Candies or chopped dry-roasted peanuts**

5 Wrap each sandwich in plastic wrap. Store sandwiches in freezer in plastic freezer bag.

Nutrition Per Sandwich: *Calories 205 (Calories from Fat 100); Fat 11g (Saturated 3g); Cholesterol 20mg; Sodium 180mg; Carbohydrate 23g (Dietary Fiber 1g); Protein 4g*

Peanut Butter Cookies (page 32), Ice-cream Sandwiches

▲▲▲▲▲ THE BEST BROWNIES ▲▲▲▲▲

24 brownies

Utensils You Will Need

Square pan, 9 × 9 × 2 inches • Pastry brush • 1-quart saucepan • Small sharp knife • Wooden spoons • Large bowl • Dry-ingredient measuring cups • Measuring spoons • Electric mixer • Pot holders • Wire cooling rack • Ruler

1 Heat oven to 350°.

2 Grease square pan with ‑ ‑ ‑ ‑ ➤ | **Shortening** |

3 Melt in saucepan over low heat, stirring a few times, then remove from heat and cool slightly ‑ ‑ ‑ ‑ ➤ | **5 ounces unsweetened chocolate**
 2/3 cup margarine or butter |

4 Beat in large bowl with electric mixer on high speed 5 minutes ‑ ‑ ‑ ‑ ➤

5 Beat the melted chocolate mixture into sugar mixture with electric mixer on low speed.

| **1 3/4 cups sugar**
 2 teaspoons vanilla
 3 large eggs |

6 Beat in until mixed ‑ ‑ ‑ ‑ ➤ | **1 cup all-purpose flour** |

7 Stir in ‑ ‑ ‑ ‑ ➤

8 Spread batter in pan.

| **1 cup chopped nuts**
 1 cup (6 ounces) semisweet chocolate chips, if you like |

9 Bake 40 to 45 minutes or just until brownies begin to pull away from sides of pan. Cool completely on wire rack.

10 Make ‑ ‑ ‑ ‑ ➤ | **Chocolate Frosting (below)** |

11 Frost brownies with frosting. Cut into 2 1/4 × 1 1/2-inch bars.

CHOCOLATE FROSTING

2-quart saucepan • Small sharp knife • Wooden spoon •
Dry-ingredient measuring cup • Measuring spoon

1 Melt in saucepan over low heat,
stirring a few times, then remove
from heat - - - - - - - - - ▶

> **2 ounces unsweetened chocolate**
> **2 tablespoons (from a stick)**
> **margarine or butter**

2 Stir in until smooth - - - - - - ▶

> **2 cups powdered sugar**
> **3 tablespoons hot water**

Nutrition Per Brownie: Calories 260 (Calories from Fat 125); Fat 14g (Saturated 4g); Cholesterol 25mg; Sodium 80mg; Carbohydrate 32g (Dietary Fiber 1g); Protein 3g

▲▲▲▲▲ DOUBLE MINT BROWNIES ▲▲▲▲▲

24 brownies

🍴 Utensils You Will Need

Rectangular pan, 13 × 9 × 2 inches • Pastry brush • Pot holders • Spatula • Wire cooling rack • Medium bowl • Eggbeater • Liquid measuring cup • Measuring spoons • Pot holders • Ruler • Sharp knife

1 Heat oven to 350°.

2 Grease bottom only of rectangular pan with ------→ **Shortening**

3 Bake in pan as directed on package for fudgelike brownies ------→ **1 package (1 lb 6.75 oz) supreme brownie mix with pouch of chocolate flavor syrup**

4 Immediately after baking, put on brownies ------→ **20 to 24 chocolate-covered peppermint patties, unwrapped**

5 Return brownies to oven for 3 to 4 minutes or until patties are softened.

6 Spread patties evenly over top of brownies with spatula. Cool completely on wire rack.

7 Cut into 2-inch squares. Cover and refrigerate any leftover brownies.

Nutrition Per Brownie: *Calories 175 (Calories from Fat 65); Fat 7g (Saturated 1g); Cholesterol 20mg; Sodium 95mg; Carbohydrate 27g (Dietary Fiber 0g); Protein 1g*

▲▲▲▲ SUPER SNACK BARS ▲▲▲▲

32 bars *(photo page 41)*

🍴 Utensils You Will Need

Large bowl • Dry-ingredient measuring cups • Small sharp knife • Measuring spoons • Wooden spoon • Rectangular pan, 13 × 9 × 2 inches • Pot holders • Wire cooling rack • Ruler • Sharp knife

1 Heat oven to 350°.

2 Grease rectangular pan with ➔ **Shortening**

3 Mix in large bowl with wooden spoon ➔
3/4 cup granulated sugar
3/4 cup packed brown sugar
3/4 cup (1 1/2 sticks) margarine or butter, softened
1 teaspoon vanilla
2 large eggs

4 Stir in ➔
2 cups all-purpose flour
1 teaspoon baking soda
1/2 teaspoon baking powder
1/2 teaspoon salt
1 cup whole-grain wheat flake cereal, slightly crushed
3/4 cup quick-cooking oats
3/4 cup chopped pecans
2/3 cup candy-coated chocolate candies

5 Spread batter in pan.

6 Sprinkle with ➔
1/3 cup candy-coated chocolate candies
1/4 cup chopped pecans

7 Bake 30 to 40 minutes or until golden brown. Cool completely on wire rack. Cut into about 2 × 1 1/4-inch bars.

Nutrition Per Bar: Calories 175 (Calories from Fat 80); Fat 9g (Saturated 2g); Cholesterol 15mg; Sodium 150mg; Carbohydrate 23g (Dietary Fiber 1g); Protein 2g

PEANUT BUTTER AND
▲▲▲▲▲ JAM BARS ▲▲▲▲▲

32 bars

⑂♌ Utensils You Will Need

Large bowl • Dry-ingredient measuring cups • Wooden spoon •
Measuring spoons • Tablespoon • Rectangular pan, 13 × 9 × 2 inches •
Pot holders • Wire cooling rack • Ruler • Sharp knife

1 Heat oven to 350°.

2 Mix in large bowl with wooden
spoon - - - - - - - - - ➤

> **1/2 cup granulated sugar**
> **1/2 cup packed brown sugar**
> **1/2 cup shortening**
> **1/2 cup peanut butter**
> **1 large egg**

3 Stir in - - - - - - - - - ➤

> **1 1/4 cups all-purpose flour**
> **3/4 teaspoon baking soda**
> **1/2 teaspoon baking powder**

4 Save 1 cup dough. Press rest of the
dough in rectangular pan.

5 Spread on dough in pan - - - - ➤

> **1/2 cup strawberry jam**

6 Crumble saved dough, then sprinkle
over jam.

7 Bake 20 to 25 minutes or until golden
brown. Cool completely on wire rack.

8 Drizzle with - - - - - - - - ➤

> **Glaze (right)**

9 Cut into about 2 × 1 1/4-inch bars.

GLAZE 1-quart saucepan • Small sharp knife •
Dry-ingredient measuring cup • Wooden spoon • Measuring spoon

1 Melt in saucepan over low heat,
then remove from heat ‑ ‑ ‑ ‑ ‑ ➤ **2 tablespoons (from a stick)
margarine or butter**

2 Mix in with wooden spoon ‑ ‑ ‑ ➤ **1 cup powdered sugar
1 teaspoon vanilla**

3 Beat in with wooden spoon,
1 teaspoon at a time, until smooth
and thin enough to drizzle ‑ ‑ ‑ ‑ ➤ **3 to 4 teaspoons hot water**

*Nutrition Per Bar: Calories 130 (Calories from Fat 55); Fat 6g (Saturated 1g);
Cholesterol 10mg; Sodium 70mg; Carbohydrate 18g (Dietary Fiber 0g); Protein 1g*

HINT
*You can use your
favorite flavor of
jam in these bars!*

▲▲▲▲▲ DOUBLE APPLE BARS ▲▲▲▲▲

24 bars

🍴 Utensils You Will Need

Large bowl • Dry-ingredient measuring cups • Wooden spoon • Measuring spoons • Tablespoon • Square pan, 9 × 9 × 2 inches • Toothpick • Pot holders • Wire cooling rack • Ruler • Sharp knife

1 Heat oven to 350°.

2 Grease rectangular pan with ‑ ‑ ‑ ➔ | **Shortening** |

3 Mix in large bowl with wooden spoon ‑ ‑ ‑ ‑ ‑ ‑ ‑ ➔

> **3/4 cup packed brown sugar**
> **3/4 cup applesauce**
> **1/4 cup vegetable oil**
> **1 large egg**

4 Stir in ‑ ‑ ‑ ‑ ‑ ‑ ‑ ➔

> **1 1/4 cups all-purpose flour**
> **1/2 teaspoon baking soda**
> **1/2 teaspoon ground cinnamon**
> **1/4 teaspoon salt**

5 Stir in ‑ ‑ ‑ ‑ ‑ ‑ ➔

> **1/2 cup chopped unpeeled all-purpose apple**

6 Spread batter in pan.

7 Bake 25 to 30 minutes or until toothpick poked in center comes out clean. Cool completely on wire rack.

8 If you like, sprinkle with ‑ ‑ ‑ ‑ ➔ | **Powdered sugar** |

9 Cut into 2 1/4 × 1 1/2-inch bars.

Nutrition Per Bar: *Calories 85 (Calories from Fat 25); Fat 3g (Saturated 1g); Cholesterol 10mg; Sodium 55mg; Carbohydrate 14g (Dietary Fiber 0g); Protein 1g*

Double Apple Bars

CHEWY FRUIT AND
▲▲▲▲▲ NUT BARS ▲▲▲▲▲

48 bars

Utensils You Will Need

Large bowl • Dry-ingredient measuring cups • Measuring spoons •
Wooden spoon • Jelly roll pan, 15 1/2 × 10 1/2 × 1 inches • Pot holders •
Wire cooling rack • Ruler • Sharp knife

1 Heat oven to 375°.

2 Mix in large bowl with wooden
spoon ▪ ▪ ▪ ▪ ▪ ▪ ▪ ▪ ▶

> **1 1/2 cups packed brown sugar**
> **1/2 cup shortening**
> **1/2 cup (1 stick) margarine or**
> **butter, softened**
> **2 large eggs**

3 Stir in ▪ ▪ ▪ ▪ ▪ ▪ ▪ ▪ ▶

> **2 cups all-purpose flour**
> **1 teaspoon baking powder**
> **1 teaspoon salt**
> **1 teaspoon ground cinnamon**

4 Stir in ▪ ▪ ▪ ▪ ▪ ▪ ▪ ▪ ▶

> **1 package (6 ounces) diced**
> **dried fruits and raisins**
> **1 cup chopped walnuts**

5 Spread batter in pan. Bake 20 to 25
minutes or until toothpick poked in
center comes out clean. Cool
completely on wire rack.

6 If you like, sprinkle with ▪ ▪ ▪ ▪ ▶

> **Powdered sugar**

7 Cut into about 2 × 1 1/2-inch bars.

Nutrition Per Bar: *Calories 115 (Calories from Fat 55); Fat 6g (Saturated 1g); Cholesterol 10mg; Sodium 85mg; Carbohydrate 14g (Dietary Fiber 1g); Protein 1g*

Mike thought these fruity bars were easy to prepare. He also thinks they would be good with chopped dates in place of the fruit bits—we agree!

2

▲▲▲▲▲▲

Creative Fun
Cakes

Chocolate Gift Loaf (page 62))

▲▲▲▲▲ **HEART CAKE** ▲▲▲▲▲

12 servings

🍴 **Utensils You Will Need**

Round pan, 8 × 1 1/2 inches • Square pan, 8 × 8 × 2 inches • Pastry brush •
Liquid measuring cup • Large bowl • Electric mixer • Pot holders •
Wire cooling racks • Large tray or covered cardboard,
18 × 15 inches • Sharp knife

1 Heat oven to 350°.

2 Grease round and square pans
with ▬ ▬ ▬ ▬ ▬ ▬ ▬ ▬ ▬ ▬ ➤

> **Shortening**

3 Put small amount in pans and
shake to coat, then pour out any
extra ▬ ▬ ▬ ▬ ▬ ▬ ▬ ▬ ➤

> **All-purpose flour**

4 Make and bake as directed on
package for 8-inch round pans,
dividing batter between round and
square pans ▬ ▬ ▬ ▬ ▬ ▬ ➤

> **1 package (1 lb 2.25 oz) white
> or sour cream white cake mix
> with pudding**

5 **Adult help:** Cool cakes in pans 10
minutes, then remove from pans to
wire rack. Cool completely.

6 Cut round cake in half, as shown in drawing. Put square cake on tray with
one point toward you. Put cut side of each half of round cake against one of
the top sides of square cake, as shown in drawing, to make a heart.

7 Make as directed on package with electric mixer ━ ━ ━ ━ ━ ━ ━ ━ ━ ➤   **1 package (7.2 ounces) fluffy white frosting mix**

8 Beat into frosting to tint pink ━ ━ ━ ➤   **Few drops of red food color**

9 Frost cake with frosting. Be sure to cover top of cake well, especially over the cut sections.

10 Decorate cake with ━ ━ ━ ━ ━ ━ ➤   **Red candies or red sugar**

Nutrition Per Serving: Calories 250 (Calories from Fat 25); Fat 3g (Saturated 1g); Cholesterol 0mg; Sodium 260mg; Carbohydrate 54g (Dietary Fiber 0g); Protein 2g

▲▲▲▲▲ MYSTERY CAKE ▲▲▲▲▲

9 servings

Utensils You Will Need

Square pan, 9 × 9 × 2 inches • Pastry brush • Large bowl •
Dry-ingredient measuring cups • Measuring spoons • Electric mixer •
Rubber scraper • Toothpick • 1 1/2-quart saucepan • Small spatula

1 Heat oven to 325°.

2 Grease square pan with – – – – – ➤ | **Shortening**

3 Put small amount in pan and shake to
coat, then pour out any extra – – – ➤ | **All-purpose flour**

4 Beat in large bowl with electric
mixer on medium speed about
30 seconds, scraping bowl all the
time, until mixed – – – – – – – ➤

> **1 1/2 cups all-purpose flour**
> **1 cup granulated sugar**
> **2 tablespoons margarine or butter, softened**
> **1 teaspoon ground cinnamon**
> **1 teaspoon baking soda**
> **1/2 teaspoon salt**
> **1/2 teaspoon ground nutmeg**
> **1/4 teaspoon ground cloves**
> **1 large egg**
> **1 can (10 3/4 ounces) condensed tomato soup**

5 Beat batter with electric mixer on high
speed 3 minutes, scraping bowl a few
times.

6 If you like, stir into batter – – – – ➤

> **1/2 cup raisins**
> **1/2 cup chopped nuts**

7 Spread batter in pan.

8 **Adult help:** Bake 37 to 43 minutes or
until toothpick poked in center comes out clean. Cool on wire rack.

9 **Adult help:** Heat in 1 1/2-quart saucepan over medium heat until light brown ▪ ▪ ▪ ▪ ▪ ▪ ▪ ▪ ▪ ▪ ▪ ➤

3 tablespoons margarine or butter

10 Beat in ▪ ▪ ▪ ▪ ▪ ▪ ▪ ▪ ▪ ▪ ▪ ➤

3/4 cup powdered sugar   **1 teaspoon vanilla**   **3 to 4 teaspoons milk**

11 Frost cake with frosting.

Nutrition Per Serving: *Calories 360 (Calories from Fat 110); Fat 12g (Saturated 2g); Cholesterol 25mg; Sodium 580mg; Carbohydrate 61g (Dietary Fiber 2g); Protein 4g*

HINT
Beat in enough milk to make frosting spreadable. If frosting becomes too stiff to spread, stir in more milk, 1/2 teaspoon at a time.

Clare's mom said that Clare was sure she wouldn't like this cake with tomato soup in it— but she loves it, and loves sharing the mystery!

▲▲▲▲ CHOCOLATE GIFT LOAF ▲▲▲▲

14 servings *(photo page 57)*

Utensils You Will Need

Sharp knife • Cutting board • 1-quart saucepan • Loaf pan, 9 × 5 × 3 inches •
Pastry brush • 2 large bowls • Dry-ingredient measuring cups •
Liquid measuring cup • Measuring spoons • Electric mixer • Rubber scraper •
Toothpick • Wire cooling rack • Small sharp knife • Small spatula •
Kitchen scissors

1 Heat oven to 350°.

2 Melt in saucepan over low heat,
stirring a few times, then remove
from heat and cool slightly ▪ ▪ ▪ ➤

> **2 ounces unsweetened
> chocolate, chopped**

3 Grease loaf pan with ▪ ▪ ▪ ▪ ➤

> **Shortening**

4 Put small amount in pan and shake to
coat, then pour out any extra ▪ ▪ ➤

> **All-purpose flour**

5 Beat in large bowl with electric mixer
on medium speed about 30 seconds,
scraping bowl all the time,
until mixed ▪ ▪ ▪ ▪ ▪ ➤

> **1 1/2 cups all-purpose flour
> 1 cup sugar
> 1/2 cup shortening
> 3/4 cup milk
> 2 teaspoons baking powder
> 1 teaspoon vanilla
> 1/2 teaspoon salt
> 2 large eggs
> The melted chocolate**

6 Beat batter with electric mixer on high
speed 3 minutes, scraping bowl a few
times. Spread batter in pan.

7 Bake 1 hour 5 minutes to 1 hour 10 minutes or until toothpick poked in center comes out clean. **Adult help:** Cool cake in pan 10 minutes, then remove from pan to wire rack. Cool completely.

8 Beat in second large bowl with electric mixer on medium speed until smooth and spreadable (if necessary, add more water, 1/2 teaspoon at a time) ‑ ‑ ‑ ‑ ‑ ‑ ➤

> **3 cups powdered sugar**
> **1/3 cup (from a stick)**
> **margarine or butter, softened**
> **1 teaspoon vanilla**
> **1 tablespoon water**

9 Frost cake with frosting

10 Cut into strips with scissors, and put on cake to look like ribbon on a wrapped package, looping strips on top for bow ‑ ‑ ‑ ‑ ‑ ‑ ‑ ➤

> **2 rolls cherry or strawberry**
> **chewy fruit snack (from 4-ounce**
> **package)**

Nutrition Per Serving: *Calories 370 (Calories from Fat 145); Fat 16g (Saturated 5g); Cholesterol 60 mg; Sodium 210mg; Carbohydrate 54g; (Dietary Fiber 1g); Protein 3g*

Amanda enjoyed the step-by-step process of making this special cake. Her family thought it looked very attractive, and she was pleased by their reaction.

COOKIE-SOUR CREAM
▲▲▲▲▲ **CAKE** ▲▲▲▲▲

8 servings

🍴 Utensils You Will Need

Round pan, 8 × 1 1/2 or 9 × 1 1/2 inches • Pastry brush • Sharp knife •
Cutting board • Large bowl • Dry-ingredient measuring cup •
Small sharp knife • Liquid measuring cup • Measuring spoons •
Electric mixer • Rubber scraper • Wooden spoon • Pot holders •
Wire cooling rack

1 Heat oven to 350°.

2 Grease round pan with ‑ ‑ ‑ ‑ ➡ | **Shortening**

3 Put small amount in pan and shake
to coat, then pour out any extra ‑ ‑ ➡ | **All-purpose flour**

4 **Adult help:** Coarsely chop with knife,
then set aside ‑ ‑ ‑ ‑ ‑ ‑ ➡ | **8 creme-filled sandwich cookies**

5 Beat in large bowl with electric
mixer on low speed 30 seconds,
scraping bowl all the time ‑ ‑ ‑ ➡

| **1 cup all-purpose flour**
3/4 cup sugar
1/2 cup sour cream
**1/4 cup (1/2 stick) margarine
or butter, softened**
1/4 cup water
1/2 teaspoon baking soda
1/2 teaspoon baking powder
1 large egg

6 Beat batter with electric mixer on high
speed 2 minutes, scraping bowl a few
times. Stir the chopped cookies into
batter. Spread batter in pan.

7 Bake 30 to 35 minutes or until cake
springs back when touched lightly in
center. **Adult help:** Cool cake in pan
10 minutes, then remove from pan to
wire rack. (See right.) Cool completely.

8 Frost cake with ‑ ‑ ‑ ‑ ‑ ‑ ➡ | **Sweetened Whipped Cream
(right)**

9 If you like, decorate cake with more
cookies.

Help for step 7.

SWEETENED WHIPPED CREAM Medium
bowl • Liquid measuring cup • Measuring spoon • Eggbeater

1 Chill medium bowl in freezer about 15 minutes or until cold.

2 Beat in chilled bowl with eggbeater
until stiff ➤

> **3/4 cup whipping (heavy) cream**
> **2 tablespoons granulated or powdered sugar**

Nutrition Per Serving: Calories 340 (Calories from Fat 160); Fat 18g (Saturated 8g); Cholesterol 60mg; Sodium 250mg; Carbohydrate 42g (Dietary Fiber 1g); Protein 4g

Sara thought frosting and decorating cake with cookies was almost as much fun as eating it! She suggests using frozen whipped topping (thawed) for the frosting in place of the whipped cream. We think that would work just great.

UPSIDE-DOWN
▲▲▲▲▲ **PINEAPPLE CAKE** ▲▲▲▲▲

9 servings *(photo page 68)*

Utensils You Will Need

Square pan, 9 × 9 × 2 inches • Small sharp knife • Pot holders •
Dry-ingredient measuring cups • Can opener • Large bowl •
Liquid measuring cup • Measuring spoons • Electric mixer •
Rubber scraper • Toothpick • Heatproof serving plate

1 Heat oven to 350°.

2 Melt in square pan in oven ‑ ‑ ‑ ‑ ▶

> **1/4 cup (1/2 stick) margarine or butter**

3 Sprinkle over margarine ‑ ‑ ‑ ‑ ‑ ▶

> **2/3 cup packed brown sugar**

4 Put on top of brown sugar mixture ‑ ▶

> **1 can (about 16 ounces) sliced pineapple, drained**

5 If you like, put in centers of pineapple slices ‑ ‑ ‑ ‑ ‑ ‑ ▶

> **Maraschino cherries**

6 Beat in large bowl with electric mixer on low speed 30 seconds, scraping bowl all the time ‑ ‑ ‑ ▶

7 Beat batter with electric mixer on high speed 3 minutes, scraping bowl a few times. Pour batter over fruit mixture in pan.

> **1 1/3 cups all-purpose flour
> 1 cup granulated sugar
> 1/3 cup shortening
> 3/4 cup milk
> 1 1/2 teaspoons baking powder
> 1/2 teaspoon salt
> 1 large egg**

8 Bake 55 to 60 minutes or until toothpick poked in center comes out clean. **Adult help:** Immediately turn pan upside down onto heatproof serving plate. Let pan remain over cake a few minutes, then remove pan.

9 Serve warm, and if you like, serve with ----------→ **Sweetened Whipped Cream (page 65)**

Nutrition Per Serving: Calories 440 (Calories from Fat 180); Fat 20g (Saturated 7g); Cholesterol 45mg; Sodium 290mg; Carbohydrate 62g (Dietary Fiber 1g); Protein 4g

HINT
If any pieces of pineapple or cherries stick to the pan when you remove it, just pick them off and place on cake where they go.

▲▲▲▲▲ CANDY BAR CUPCAKES ▲▲▲▲▲

About 20 cupcakes

🍴 Utensils You Will Need

Muffin pan with medium cups, 2 1/2 × 1 1/4 inches • Pastry brush •
Cutting board • Sharp knife • Large bowl • Liquid measuring cup •
Electric mixer • Pot holders • Wire cooling rack

1 **Adult help:** Coarsely chop all the candy, then finely chop enough to measure 3/4 cup - - - - - - →

> **8 bars (2.1 ounces each) chocolate-covered crispy peanut-buttery candy**

2 Make and bake cupcakes as directed on package—except after beating, gently stir in the 3/4 cup finely chopped candy - - - - - - →

> **1 package (1 lb 2.25 oz) white cake mix with pudding**

3 **Adult help:** Immediately remove cupcakes from pan to wire rack. Cool completely.

4 Frost cupcakes with - - - - - - →

> **1 tub (1 lb) milk chocolate ready-to-spread frosting**

5 Put coarsely chopped candy pieces on tops of cupcakes. Store loosely covered at room temperature.

Nutrition Per Cupcake: Calories 330 (Calories from Fat 135); Fat 15g (Saturated 10g); Cholesterol 5mg; Sodium 250mg; Carbohydrate 46g (Dietary Fiber 1g); Protein 4g

HINT
Candy bars are easier to cut if refrigerated about 1 hour.

Upside-down Pineapple Cake (page 66)

▲▲▲▲▲ BANANA-OATMEAL CAKE ▲▲▲▲▲

15 servings

Utensils You Will Need

Rectangular pan, 13 × 9 × 2 inches • Pastry brush • Large bowl •
Liquid measuring cup • Dry-ingredient measuring cups • Fork •
Measuring spoons • Wooden spoon • Pot holders • Toothpick •
Wire cooling rack

1 Heat oven to 350°.

2 Grease rectangular pan with ‑ ‑ ‑ ➤ | **Shortening** |

3 Beat in large bowl with wooden
spoon ‑ ‑ ‑ ‑ ‑ ‑ ‑ ‑ ➤

> **1 1/2 cups mashed very ripe bananas (4 medium)**
> **3/4 cup sugar**
> **2/3 cup vegetable oil**
> **2/3 cup buttermilk**
> **1 teaspoon vanilla**
> **1 large egg**

4 Mix in ‑ ‑ ‑ ‑ ‑ ‑ ‑ ‑ ➤

> **1 1/3 cups all-purpose flour**
> **1 cup quick-cooking or regular oats**
> **2 teaspoons baking soda**
> **1 1/2 teaspoons ground cinnamon**
> **1 teaspoon baking powder**
> **1/2 teaspoon ground cloves**

5 Stir in ‑ ‑ ‑ ‑ ‑ ‑ ‑ ➤

> **2/3 cup chopped nuts**
> **2/3 cup raisins**

6 Spread batter in pan.

7 Bake 30 to 35 minutes or until toothpick poked in center comes out clean. Cool completely on wire rack.

8 If you like, sprinkle with – – – – ➞ | **Powdered sugar**

Nutrition Per Serving: Calories 275 (Calories from Fat 125); Fat 14g (Saturated 2g); Cholesterol 15mg; Sodium 220mg; Carbohydrate 35g (Dietary Fiber 2g); Protein 4g

Kirsten thought it was fun for a kid like her to make a cake all by herself and let people try it. She chose to leave the raisins out.

▲▲▲▲▲ JELLY ROLL ▲▲▲▲▲

10 servings

🍴 Utensils You Will Need

Jelly roll pan, 15 1/2 × 10 1/2 × 1 inch • Aluminum foil • Pastry brush •
Medium mixer bowl • Electric mixer • Dry-ingredient measuring cups •
Liquid measuring cup • Measuring spoons • Toothpick • Pot holders •
Clean kitchen towel • Sharp knife • Wire cooling rack • Fork • Knife

1 Heat oven to 375°. Line jelly roll pan with aluminum foil.

2 Generously grease foil with → → → → → **Shortening**

3 Beat in medium bowl with electric mixer on high speed about 5 minutes or until thick and lemon-colored → → **3 large eggs**

4 Beat in, a little at a time → → → → → **1 cup granulated sugar**

5 Beat in on low speed → → → → → → **1/3 cup water**
1 teaspoon vanilla

6 Beat in, a little at a time, just until batter is smooth → → → → → → → **1 cup cake flour or 3/4 cup all-purpose flour**
1 teaspoon baking powder
1/4 teaspoon salt

7 Pour batter into pan, spreading to corners.

8 Bake 12 to 15 minutes or until toothpick poked in center comes out clean.

9 Sprinkle towel generously with → → → **Powdered sugar**

10 Adult help: Immediately after baking, loosen cake from edges of pan and turn upside down onto towel. Carefully remove foil. Trim off edges of cake if they are very crisp so that cake will not split when rolled.

11 Adult help: While hot, carefully roll cake and towel from narrow end. Cool on wire rack at least 30 minutes. Unroll cake and remove towel.

12 Beat with fork just enough to soften, then spread over cake ▰ ▰ ▰ ▰ ▰ ➤ | **About 2/3 cup jelly or jam**

13 Roll up cake, then sprinkle with ▰ ▰ ➤ | **Powdered sugar**

Nutrition Per Serving: *Calories 215 (Calories from Fat 20); Fat 2g (Saturated 1g); Cholesterol 65 mg; Sodium 130mg; Carbohydrate 46g (Dietary Fiber 0g); Protein 3g*

Justin was very pleased with his finished cake and thought it looked like something from a bakery— and it tasted good too!

▲▲▲▲▲ MINIATURE LOGS ▲▲▲▲▲

About 14 logs

Utensils You Will Need

Large bowl • Liquid measuring cups • Rubber scraper •
Muffin pan with medium cups, 2 1/2 × 1 1/4 inches • Pastry brush •
Pot holders • Wire cooling rack • Knife • Fork • Rolling pin • Sharp knife

1 Make and bake 28 cupcakes as
directed on ➤ **1 package (1 lb 2.25 oz) devil's food cake mix with pudding**

2 **Adult help:** Immediately remove cupcakes from pan to wire rack. Cool completely.

3 Remove paper baking cups if you
used them.

4 Make ➤ **Creamy Chocolate Frosting (right)**

5 Put 2 cupcakes together end to end, as
shown in drawing, with a small amount
of frosting. Frost sides of logs, leaving
ends unfrosted. Make strokes in frosting
with fork to look like bark.

6 Sprinkle generously on breadboard ➤ **Sugar**

7 Roll in sugar into 1/8-inch-thick
ovals ➤ **14 large red gumdrops**

8 Cut hatchets from ovals, as shown in drawing. Wipe kitchen knife on wet sponge between hatchets. Put a gumdrop hatchet on each log.

CREAMY CHOCOLATE FROSTING
1-quart saucepan • Wooden spoon • Large bowl • Electric mixer •
Dry-ingredient measuring cups • Measuring spoons

1 Melt in saucepan over low heat, stirring a few times, then remove from heat and cool slightly ➜ **3 ounces unsweetened chocolate**

2 Mix in large bowl with electric mixer on medium speed ➜ **The melted chocolate / 1/2 cup (1 stick) margarine or butter, softened**

3 Stir in ➜ **3 cups powdered sugar**

4 Beat in with electric mixer on medium speed until smooth and spreadable ➜ **2 teaspoons vanilla / About 3 tablespoons milk**

Nutrition Per Log: *Calories 355 (Calories from Fat 115); Fat 13g (Saturated 4g); Cholesterol 0mg; Sodium 410mg; Carbohydrate 60g (Dietary Fiber 2g); Protein 2g*

STRAWBERRY PIE ▲▲▲▲▲

8 servings

Utensils You Will Need

2 medium bowls • Dry-ingredient measuring cups • Measuring spoons • Fork •
Pastry blender • Pastry cloth and cloth cover for rolling pin • Rolling pin •
Pie plate, 9 × 1 1/2 inches • Colander • Sharp knife • Potato masher •
Pot holders • Wire cooling rack • 1 1/2-quart saucepan •
Liquid measuring cup • Wooden spoon

1 Heat oven to 475°.

2 Mix in medium bowl with fork - - ➤

> **1 cup all-purpose flour**
> **1/2 teaspoon salt**

3 Cut into flour mixture with pastry
blender until pieces are the size of
small peas - - - - - - - - - ➤

> **1/3 cup plus 1 tablespoon
> shortening**

4 Sprinkle in, 1 tablespoon at a time,
tossing with fork until all the flour is
wet and pastry almost leaves side of
bowl - - - - - - - - - - - ➤

> **2 to 3 tablespoons cold water**

5 Cover a breadboard with a pastry
cloth. Sprinkle flour lightly over cloth. Shape pastry into a ball on floured
cloth. Shape ball into a flattened round. Roll pastry with floured cloth-
covered rolling pin until pastry is 2 inches larger than pie plate
turned upside down.

6 Fold pastry into fourths. Put pastry in pie plate. Unfold and fit pastry into
plate, pressing firmly against bottom and side. Trim edge of pastry that
hangs over pie plate to 1 inch from rim of plate. Fold and roll pastry under,
even with pie plate, then press around edge with fork dipped in flour. Poke
bottom and side of pastry many times with fork.

7 Bake 8 to 10 minutes or until crust is light brown. Cool completely on wire
rack.

8 Wash in colander, then remove stems from ▪ ▪ ▪ ▪ ▪ ▪ ▪ ▪ ▪ ➤ | **6 cups whole strawberries**

9 Mash 2 cups of the strawberries in medium bowl with potato masher or fork to measure 1 cup mashed strawberries. Save the rest of the strawberries for step #14.

10 Mix in saucepan with wooden spoon ▪ ▪ ▪ ▪ ▪ ▪ ▪ ▪ ▪ ➤ | **1 cup sugar**
2 tablespoons cornstarch

11 Stir in ▪ ▪ ▪ ▪ ▪ ▪ ▪ ▪ ➤ | **The mashed strawberries**
1/2 cup water

12 **Adult help:** Cook sugar-strawberry mixture over medium-high heat, stirring all the time, until mixture thickens and boils. Boil and stir 1 minute, then cool.

13 Beat until smooth with wooden spoon, then spread over bottom of pie crust ▪ ▪ ▪ ▪ ▪ ▪ ▪ ➤ | **1 package (3 ounces) cream cheese, softened**

14 Pile whole strawberries on cream cheese in pie crust. Pour cooked strawberry mixture over top. Refrigerate about 2 hours or until set. Cover and refrigerate any leftover pie.

Here's another idea. . . Make **Raspberry Pie**: Use 6 cups raspberries in place of the strawberries.

Nutrition Per Serving: Calories 320 (Calories from Fat 125); Fat 14g (Saturated 5g); Cholesterol 10mg; Sodium 170mg; Carbohydrate 47g (Dietary Fiber 2g); Protein 3g